CULINARY BLISS:

Authentic Cajun French and Mediterranean Cuisine

Michelle Ackal Dabdoub

Photography: Nancy Farrar, Farrar Food Photography
Design & Layout: Laura Kayata, SPARK Creative Services

TABOULA

serves 6-8

INGREDIENTS

1 cup fine cracked wheat (#2 wheat)

2 bunches green onions

1 carton cherry tomatoes or 4 large tomatoes

3/4 cup of fresh-squeezed lemon juice

1 bunch parsley (chopped fine, stems removed)

2 large English cucumbers chopped

1/2 cup dried mint (from spice section in grocery)

3/4 cup cold-pressed olive oil

Salt and pepper to taste

Red pepper (optional) to give extra spice

INSTRUCTIONS

Wash wheat in cold water and soak for 1-2 hours in the refrigerator.

Once all of the water is absorbed and wheat has expanded, squeeze wheat with your hands to drain out excess water.

Mix with chopped onions, tomatoes, parsley and cucumbers.

Add fresh lemon juice and olive oil. Add salt and pepper.

Serve as a salad, or inside a lettuce wrap or a pocket of whole wheat pita bread.

FATOOSH SALAD

serves 6-8

INGREDIENTS

4 loaves whole wheat pita bread

3 large tomatoes

2 English cucumbers

1 bunch green onions, chopped

1 bunch parsley, chopped

1/2 cup dried mint leaves

DRESSING

1/2 cup lemon juice

3/4 cup cold-pressed olive oil

4 cloves fresh garlic, crushed

salt and pepper to taste

INSTRUCTIONS

Toast whole wheat pita bread until golden brown then break into pieces.

Chop all of the salad ingredients and combine in a bowl.

Combine the dressing ingredients (left). Pout over the chopped ingredients and mix well.

Serve immediately.

CUCUMBER AND YOGURT SALAD

serves
6-8

INGREDIENTS

2 English cucumbers, peeled and chopped

2 garlic cloves, crushed

1 small jar or 1.2 of large jar nonfat Bulgarian yogurt (Whole Foods)

1-2 tbsp of dried mint leaves

INSTRUCTIONS

Crush fresh garlic with salt and pepper. Pour yogurt slowly into bowl and add cucumbers and mint leaves.

Refrigerate for 1-2 hours and serve.

serves 8

SYRIAN SALAD
a Lebanese favorite!

INGREDIENTS

2 bunches Romaine lettuce

2 large or 1 pkg cherry tomatoes

1 English cucumber

1 avocado, peeled and sliced

3 mini peppers: red, yellow, orange

3 cloves fresh garlic

3/4 cup cold-pressed olive oil

1/2 cup fresh lemon juice

1/2 cup dried mint leaves

1/2 tsp each: salt and fresh pepper

INSTRUCTIONS

Wash and cut lettuce leaves. Dry well with paper towels.

Mash fresh garlic with salt and pepper in a wooden bowl. Add lemon juice and olive oil.

Add the chopped vegetables and top with dried mint leaves.

Mix well and serve immediately.

AVOCADO SALAD

serves
4-6

INGREDIENTS

2 avocados, peeled and sliced

1/4 cup of green onions, chopped

2 tbsp of cold pressed olive oil

1 tbsp of freshly-squeezed lemon juice

Salt and pepper to taste

INSTRUCTIONS

Combine all of the above ingredients, toss lightly and enjoy.

This is a fabulous salad that goes well with most entrees.

HUMMUS

serves
8

INGREDIENTS

2 16-ounce cans chick peas (also called garbanzos)

1 cup tahini sauce (recipe pg 11)

Lemon juice

INSTRUCTIONS

Boil chick peas and juice for 5-10 mins on medium heat. Drain.

Place chick peas and tahini sauce in food processor. Puree for 2 minutes, until smooth. More lemon may be added if needed.

Refrigerate. Garnish with paprika and a little olive oil on top.

BABA GA NOOJ

serves
4-6

INGREDIENTS

2 large eggplants

Lemon juice

1/2 cup Tahini Sauce (recipe page 11, or available at any Mediterranean Grocery)

Olive oil, pine nuts, parsley, paprika (for garnish)

INSTRUCTIONS

Poke holes in eggplant and broil in oven until soft.

When tender, run under cool water, peel and cut lengthwise.

Drain in colander and add a little lemon juice to maintain eggplant's color. Remove seeds and discard.

Mash eggplants and add tahini sauce. Mix well.

Add water if too thick - the mixture should be a dip consistency.

Garnish with olive oil, pine nuts, parsley and paprika.

LENTIL SOUP

serves 4-6

INGREDIENTS

2 cups dried lentils

2 quarts water

2 cups celery, chopped

3 large onions, slivered

1 cup carrots, chopped

1 cup cold-pressed olive oil

2 tsp salt

4 cloves garlic, mashed

3 tbsp lemon juice

INSTRUCTIONS

Wash lentils well and place in pot with water. Cover and boil until tender. Lower heat and add remaining ingredients.

Cook until all veggies are done and soup thickens. You can add water as needed if too thick. More salt and lemon juice may be added as needed.

YOGURT AND ZATAR DIP

makes 2 cups

INGREDIENTS

2 cups plain yogurt

1 clove garlic, mashed

1/4 cup mint, chopped fine

1/4 cup parsley

1 tbsp zatar (dried herb mixture available at Mediterranean grocery)

INSTRUCTIONS

Combine all ingredients, blending well.

Serve with pita chips.

CLARIFIED BUTTER

makes 2 jars

INGREDIENTS

4-5 pounds unsalted butter (preferably Land O Lakes (R))

2 large glass jars with lids (32 oz)

INSTRUCTIONS

Place blocks of butter in deep pot on low heat. As butter melts and comes to a light boil, begin to skim the top with a spoon and put waste in a small bowl. Continue this for the next 2 hours until no more of waste from the butter floats to top.

Once the butter is clear, set aside to cool. When cool, pour into jars. Put lids on the next day.

Store in a dry cool place. Can be used in any of these recipes as a healthier option. Also, great when scrambling or frying eggs or egg whites.

TAHINI SAUCE

makes 2 cups

INGREDIENTS

1 cup tahini (available at Mediterranean grocery stores)

1 clove garlic, mashed

1 tsp salt to taste

1/2 cup cold water

1/2 cup lemon juice

INSTRUCTIONS

Mix tahini, garlic and salt in a bowl, or in processor. Add water, lemon juice and mix well until creamy. Add a little water or lemon juice if it's too thick. Adjust salt as needed. Refrigerate.

Tahini Sauce can be used with fresh asparagus, broccoli, cabbage, and fish.

serves
8-10

CABBAGE ROLLS

INGREDIENTS

2 small heads cabbage

Meat filling (recipe below)

3 cloves fresh garlic

1½ cups free-range, low sodium chicken broth

Salt to taste

1 cup fresh lemon juice

1/2 cup dried mint leaves

MEAT FILLING

1-2 pounds grass-fed beef or ground turkey

1½ sticks of butter (important ingredient - don't use less!)

Uncooked rice - 2 cups medium grain rice per pound of meat used

1 tsp each cinnamon and allspice

Salt and pepper to taste

INSTRUCTIONS

Boil water. Use 2 pots for 2 heads of cabbage. Wash cabbage, and core out the bottom, so leaves separate during cooking. Place in boiling water. Once leaves are tender, use a fork to remove them. Lay them on a cookie sheet lined with wax paper. Allow them to cool. Remove the hard ribs from each leaf so they are easier to roll.

Prepare meat mixture (left). Place one heaping spoonful of meat mixture in each leaf and roll - don't overstuff, as the meat mixture swells during cooking. Once rolled, you can slice off any excess on the ends.

Place rolls in bottom of pot and continue this process until all the leaves have been rolled. Add sliced garlic cloves between the layers. Sprinkle dried mint leaves on top. Place a small saucer on top of rolls. Add chicken broth to cover the top layer of cabbage rolls. (Cabbage produces water so you don't want them to become too soggy). Add lemon juice and salt on top. Bring to a boil, then lower the heat and cover. Let cook for 45 minutes and remove the saucer. Cook for another 30 minutes until rolls are done.

NOTE: Make sure to check while cooking, as you don't want liquid to evaporate. You can always add more liquid. Be cautious when adding chicken broth and lemon juice. You can also add more salt if you need.

GRAPE LEAVES (DOLMAS)

serves
10–12

INGREDIENTS

1 jar grape leaves(available at most stores)

Meat mixture (recipe pg. 12)

1½ cups free-range, low sodium chicken broth

1/2 cup lemon juice

Salt to taste

INSTRUCTIONS

Wash and rinse grape leaves, cut off the stems.

Line bottom of pot with 2-3 leaves. Add a tablespoon of stuffing onto the leaf lengthwise. Roll the leaves by folding in the sides and roll the leaf up tight.

Place in bottom of pot until all the leaves are rolled. Place a small saucer on top of leaves. Add chicken broth and lemon juice until it cover top of saucer. Add salt as needed. Cook for one hour or until leaves and rice are tender.

STUFFED BELL PEPPER HALVES

serves
4-6

INGREDIENTS

6 peppers cut into halves

2 pounds grass-fed beef

3 slices whole grain bread (soak in water)

1 large onion, chopped

2 cloves minced garlic

Salt and pepper

Olive oil (3 Tbsp)

INSTRUCTIONS

Brown beef in olive oil.

Add onion, garlic, salt and pepper.

Place pepper halves in glass baking dish, add ½ cup of water and steam in oven for 5 mins at 375 degrees. Discard water. Stuff the halves with meat mixture and sprinkle with bread crumbs. Add a little water to the pan and bake at 375 degrees until brown on top, for 1 hour. Cover and continue baking for 15-20 minutes.

KOUSA MIHSHEE (STUFFED BELL PEPPERS, EGGPLANT AND SQUASH)

serves
6-8

INGREDIENTS

2 green or red bell peppers

2 eggplant

2 squash

Meat mixture (recipe pg. 12)

2 cans tomato paste

Pinch raw sugar

Salt to taste

INSTRUCTIONS

Wash all vegetables. Core squash and eggplant; cut off tops of bell peppers and remove seeds. Stuff the vegetables with meat mixture. Place in 2 pots.

Cover with water, add one can of tomato paste to each pot. Add salt and a pinch of raw sugar to each. Bring to a boil, then lower heat and cover. Add more seasoning (salt, pepper, cinnamon and allspice) as desired. Cook for approximately one hour or until vegetables are tender.

This dish pairs well with Syrian Salad (page 6).

GRANDMA EDNA'S SWEET PEAS AND GROUND MEAT

serves
4-6

INGREDIENTS

1 pound grass-fed beef

2 cans tomato sauce

2 cans petite sweet peas

1 onion

Salt, pepper, cinnamon and all-spice to taste

1½ cups converted long grain rice

1/2 cup uncooked vermicelli

INSTRUCTIONS

Brown ground beef, add onions and cook.

Add the tomato sauce and 2 cans of water. Cook for approximately 20 minures, then add the peas. Season with spices and cook for another 20 minutes.

Brown vermicelli in clarified butter then cook with rice.

Cook rice according to package.

Pair with Syrian Salad (recipe pg. 6)

CHICKEN & SALMON KEBABS

serves
6–8

INGREDIENTS

3 large organic chicken breasts

3 6-oz Atlantic salmon fillets

Sea salt and black pepper

1 lemon

1 purple onion

1 red bell pepper

1 orange bell pepper

INSTRUCTIONS

Cut chicken into cubes and skewer. Grill until done.

Slice vegetables and skewer. Salt and pepper well. Grill for 20 minutes or so until done.

Cut salmon into cubes and skewer. Season with salt and pepper and a squeeze of lemon. Grill for 10 minutes.

Pairs well with Toni's Rice Dressing (page 36) and Avocado Salad (page 7).

KAFTA PATTIES

serves
4

INGREDIENTS

1 pound grass-fed beef

salt/pepper

1/2 cup dried mint leaves

1 onion, chopped very fine

1 cup fresh parsley, chopped very fine

INSTRUCTIONS

Mix meat with salt, pepper and dried mint. Add onion and fresh parsley.

Pat out into individual 3" oval patties and place on grill or in a large nonstick skillet.

Cook until done. Serve with green vegetable, sweet potato and Syrian Salad, (page 6).

BAKED FISH WITH TAHINI

serves
4

INGREDIENTS

2 pounds fresh cod or sole fillets

Salt and pepper (1 tsp of each)

1/2 - 3/4 cup cold-pressed olive oil, divided

2 medium onions, sliced

2 cups Tahini Sauce (recipe page 11)

INSTRUCTIONS

Wash and pat dry fish fillets. Place fillets in a 9x12" glass baking dish. Season with salt and pepper.

Coat each piece with olive oil.

Use the remaining olive oil to cook sliced onions until translucent. Mix tahini sauce into the onions.

Cover fish fillets with tahini sauce and onions and bake at 350 for 30 minutes. Serve with fresh green beans and avocado salad (page 7).

LAHEM MESHWI (MEAT WITH ONIONS IN BLACK IRON SKILLET)

serves
8

INGREDIENTS

2 pounds sirloin or chicken breasts

Salt, pepper and cinnamon

2 large onions, slivered

1½ tbsp butter

INSTRUCTIONS

Slice meat into strips.

Trim any excess fat from meat. Melt butter in black iron skillet. Add meat, salt, pepper and cinnamon (cover meat well with cinnamon). Add slivered onions. Cook until meat and onions are tender.

Serve with vermicelli rice and Syrian salad. (page 6). You can also serve in a whole wheat pita bread.

LAMB LOLLIPOPS

serves 4-6

INGREDIENTS

10 lamb lollipops

Allegro (R) Marinade (usually near the Worcestershire sauce)

Worcestershire sauce

Salt and pepper

Dried parsley flakes

INSTRUCTIONS

Marinate lamb in salt, pepper, Worcestershire, Allegro and parsley flakes for 3 hours.

Grill or broil in oven until pink in center. Do not overcook.

NOTE: Pair with baked sweet potato, or zucchini sauteed in olive oil.

LEMON CHICKEN

serves
6-8

INGREDIENTS

1 whole free-range chicken, cut up

Salt and pepper

1½ cup cold-pressed olive oil

3-4 fresh lemons, sliced

INSTRUCTIONS

Rinse chicken pieces and dry. Season with salt and pepper. Flash-fry chicken in olive oil, just to brown - not cook. Drain well. Place pieces in 9x13 glass baking dish. Arrange lemon slices on each piece of chicken. Add a little water or chicken broth to pan. Tent with foil, bake at 350 degrees for 30 minutes. Remove foil and bake another 15 minutes until edges of chicken are crisp. NOTE: Pair with Toni's Rice Dressing (page 36), green vegetable of your choice and a salad.

SITIE QUINNIE'S OVEN STEW

serves 4-6

INGREDIENTS

1 - 1½ pounds grass fed stew meat or sirloin, cut into pieces

1½ cup celery, diced

1 cup carrots, cut round

1½ cups russet or red new potatoes, diced

1 large onion, sliced

1½ cup cabbage, sliced

1 15-oz can tomato sauce

1 15-oz can diced tomatoes

INSTRUCTIONS

Place meat in large roaster or Dutch oven. Let meat braise in 350 degree oven while you prepare vegetables.

Place all the vegetables over the meat and stir well. Add one can of tomato sauce and one can of diced tomatoes. Stir, add salt and pepper to taste.

Put in oven and cook for 1 hour, until vegetables are tender.

serves 6-8

TURKEY MEATLOAF

INGREDIENTS

2 pounds ground turkey

1 egg

1/2 cup plain bread breads

Salt and pepper to taste

INSTRUCTIONS

Combine all ingredients.

Place in a glass baking dish and bake at 350 degrees for 45 minutes.

Pair with baked sweet potatoes or Middle Eastern Green Beans (page 38) and a salad.

SFEIHA

INGREDIENTS

2 small cans flaky biscuits
1½ lb grass fed beef
2 small onions, chopped fine
2 green bell peppers, diced
2 red bell peppers, diced
1 tsp cinnamon
1 tsp allspice
1/3 cup clarified or regular butter
1 tsp each: salt and pepper

INSTRUCTIONS

Hashwa: Saute onion in butter until translucent in medium pot. Add meat and seasonings. Cook covered until all moisture is absorbed, about 30 minutes. Set aside and let cool.

Preheat oven to 350 degrees. Remove biscuits from cans and flatten out. Add a heaping tea-spoonful of hashwa on top of biscuit. Sprinkle with diced green and red bell peppers. Place on a greased cookie sheet and bake for 20-25 mins or until golden brown.

serves
8 – 10

MEAT AND GREEN BEAN STEW (YAKHNEE)

INGREDIENTS

1 large onion, slivered

1 tbsp clarified butter

2 pounds sirloin or lean cut of meat, cubed

1 tsp salt, cinnamon

1/2 tsp of allspice

5 cloves garlic

one pound fresh green beans

2 cans tomato sauce

2 cups water, divided

INSTRUCTIONS

Saute onion in clarified butter until translucent.

Add meat and spices and cook until meat is brown. Add 1½ cups of water.

Add tomato sauce, garlic and remaining water.

Rinse and pinch off tips of green beans, add to sauce. Cook until beans are tender.

Serve over Rice Pilaf (recipe page 35).

RUZ BI DFEEN (CHICKEN & RICE)

serves
6-8

INGREDIENTS

8-10 chicken tenders, cubed

1 can garbanzo beans (chickpeas)

1 cup converted long grain rice

1 tsp each: salt, pepper, cinnamon, allspice (more if desired)

1 stick butter or ½ cup of clarified butter (See recipe on pg x)

1 large onion, sliced thin

2 cups cage-free, low sodium chicken broth

Bulgarian Yogurt (for garnish)

INSTRUCTIONS

Soak rice in hot water for 20 minutes.

In a large deep pot, brown chicken. Season with spices. Add onions and cook for approximately 15 minutes.

Rinse beans (chickpeas). Add beans and rice and cook for an additional 10 minutes. Heat chicken broth for 1 minute in microwave and add to rice mixture, stir. Cook on low heat covered until done. Stir with a fork and serve hot. Top with a teaspoon of Bulgarian Yogurt.

GRILLED PORK TENDERLOIN

serves
4-6

INGREDIENTS

Pork Tenderloin (package of 2)

Cajun Spice

Marinade (below)

MARINADE:

Tamari, Worcestershire sauce, Zesty Italian Dressing, Allegra Marinade, Parsley Flakes

INSTRUCTIONS

Sprinkle Cajun Spice on tenderloins.

Combine ingredients for marinade. Pour over pork and marinate for 2 hours in fridge.

Grill until slightly pink in center.

Serve with Grilled Veggies (page 38) and Rice Pilaf (page 35).

ITALIAN CHICKEN BREASTS

serves
4

INGREDIENTS

4 large chicken breasts

1/2 cup butter

Salt and pepper to taste

1/2 tsp garlic powder

2 cups Italian bread crumbs

INSTRUCTIONS

Preheat oven to 350 degrees. Rinse chicken and pat dry. Mix seasonings and bread crumbs together. Melt butter. Dip chicken in butter then into bread crumb mixture.

Cover a cookie sheet with foil and spray with nonstick spray. Place battered chicken on cookie sheet. Bake for 40-45 minutes. Serve with steamed veggies and salad.

CAULIFLOWER ON A BROWN GRAVY

serves
6-8

INGREDIENTS

2 pkg frozen cauliflower

2 onion, chopped

1 bell pepper, chopped

1 pound sirloin steak

2-3 cloves garlic

1 tbsp cold-pressed olive oil

Salt and pepper to taste

INSTRUCTIONS

Saute onion and bell pepper and set aside. Brown steak in iron skillet. In a separate pot, brown the cauliflower in olive oil. Add a little water, drain well. Transfer cauliflower to a big pot. Add approximately 1 cup of water to meat. Place pot on medium heat (add more water if needed). Cook for about 30 minutes or until meat is tender. Combine meat and cauliflower in big pot and cook for 10 more minutes.

Serve over rice with a green salad.

EDNA'S MACARONI CASSEROLE

serves
6-8

INGREDIENTS

1½ pounds ground turkey or beef

1 large onion

1 tbsp butter

1-2 small cans tomato sauce

1/2 can diced tomatoes

1 pkg elbow macaroni

1 pkg shredded cheddar cheese

INSTRUCTIONS

Saute onions in butter. Add ground turkey and brown.

Add tomato sauce, one can of water, salt and pepper. Cook for about 25 minutes. Spray non-stick spray in 9x13" dish and add mixture over cooked pasta and stir in the cheese.

Tent with foil and bake in 350 degree oven for 30 minutes, until bubbly.

CHICKEN TETRAZZINI

serves
12-14

INGREDIENTS

4 large cage free chicken breasts

1 8-oz pkg brown rice spaghetti

1 4-oz jar diced pimentos

1 stick butter

2 cups flour

1 can Cream of Mushroom soup
(low fat version)

1½ cup organic skim milk

1 medium onion, diced

1 8-oz can sliced water chestnuts
(optional)

2 can sliced mushrooms

1 4½-oz can sliced black olives

Garlic powder, salt, pepper to
taste

1 lb pepper cheese

INSTRUCTIONS

Boil chicken in large pot for approximately 45 minutes.

When done, remove chicken. Save water for boiling pasta. When cool, debone and cut chicken into pieces.

Melt butter in large skillet, add onions and saute.

Stir in flour, add milk, add can of soup and cheese.

Melt cheese slowly so it won't scorch. Once cheese has melted, add chicken, spices and rest of ingredients. Pour into a metal pan or casserole dish and cover.

Top with grated parmesan cheese and bake at 350 degrees for about 20 minutes until bubbly.

Serve with Syrian Salad (page 6) and a multi-grain garlic baguette.

CHICKEN OR LAMB PITA SANDWICH

serves
5

INGREDIENTS

2 pounds organic chicken breasts or lamb

2 medium onions, slivered

2 bell peppers (red, green, yellow or orange), slivered

1/4 cup margarine

Salt, pepper, cinnamon, allspice

1/4 cup water

1/2 cup tahini sauce or hummus

whole wheat pita bread

INSTRUCTIONS

Season meat with spices then slice chicken lengthwise.

Saute chicken in margarine and add onions and bell peppers. Cook until chicken is done and veggies tender.

Cut pita bread in half and add chicken.

Top with Hummus (page 7) or Tahini Sauce (page 11).

serves
4-6

JADRA (LENTILS WITH RICE)

INGREDIENTS

1 cup lentils

1/2 cup rice

4 cups water, divided

3 large onions, slivered

1/2 cup olive oil

1 tsp salt

INSTRUCTIONS

Soak rice in boiling water for 20 minutes. Rinse and drain rice, add to saucepan with 3 cups water. Add lentils. Cook, covered, on low heat until rice and lentils are tender.

Cook onions in olive oil until dark brown. Remove half the onions and set aside for garnish.Mash onions in pan with spoon. Add 1 cup water to pan and simmer. Add salt, continue cooking. Add onions to rice-lentil mixture. Cook until all water is absorbed and all ingredients are soft. Add more water if needed. Serve hot.

SPINACH MADELEINE

serves
6-8

INGREDIENTS

2 pkgs frozen chopped spinach

2 tbsp organic rice flour

3 tbsp butter

2 tbsp chopped onions

1/2 cup evaporated milk

1/2 cup liquid reserved from spinach

1/2 tsp black pepper

1/4 tsp cayenne pepper

3/4 tsp each: celery salt, garlic salt

1 6-oz pkg hot pepper cheese

1 tsp Worcestershire Sauce

1/2 cup plain bread crumbs

INSTRUCTIONS

Preheat oven to 350 degrees. Defrost spinach in microwave. Drain and reserve ½ cup of liquid from packages. In a saucepan, melt butter over low heat. Stir in flour and whisk until smooth. Add onion and cook until soft. Stir in milk and spinach slowly to avoid lumps. Cook until smooth and thick.

Add peppers, salts, cheese and Worcestershire sauce. Stir until cheese is melted. Stir in spinach.

Pour into a pan greased with coconut oil or non-stick spray. Bake for 30 minutes.

Sprinkle bread crumbs on top and bake another 5 minutes, until browned. **This side dish goes well with Lamb Lollipops (page 22) Pork Tenderloin (page 29) or chicken.**

RICE PILAF

INGREDIENTS

2 cups converted long grain rice

4 cups water or chicken broth

1 tbsp Clarified butter

Salt to taste

8 sticks uncooked vermicelli, broken into small pieces

INSTRUCTIONS

Brown vermicelli in clarified butter (Instructions, page 11).

Cook rice according to package, add vermicelli.

Salt rice as desired. Fluff with fork before serving.

BAKED BRUSSELS SPROUTS (OR ASPARAGUS)

INGREDIENTS

1 bag small Brussel sprout

1½ tbsp cold-pressed olive oil

salt and pepper to taste

INSTRUCTIONS

Rinse Brussels sprouts well.

Cut the bottoms off of the sprouts and place on foil-covered cookie sheet. Add olive oil, salt and pepper. Toss well. Bake in a 400 degree oven for about 20 minutes. Make sure to watch them - don't let them burn. Works well for fresh asparagus, too!

TONI'S RICE DRESSING

serves 6-8

INGREDIENTS

1½ cups long grain rice
1 can Beef Consomme Soup
1 can French Onion Soup
1 can water
1/2 stick butter
1 can mushroom pieces and stems

INSTRUCTIONS

Combine all the ingredients. Stir well.

Bake in a 2-quart oval baking dishat 350 degrees for 30 minutes uncovered. Cover and cook for another 15 mins.

Serve hot.

Pair with Syrian Salad (page 6).

GRILLED VEGETABLES

serves
4-6

INGREDIENTS

1 yellow bell pepper, slivered

1 red bell pepper, slivered

1 purple onion, slivered

Asparagus, cut bottoms

1 zucchini, sliced

1/2 cup cold-pressed olive oil

Salt and pepper to taste

INSTRUCTIONS

Wash all vegetables and prepare as stated above. Place in foil, add olive oil, salt and pepper and toss well.

Wrap well and place directly on grill. Let cook for approximately 15 minutes.

This side goes well with grilled fish, chicken and red meats.

AUNT MAE HELEN'S RICE DRESSING

serves
8-10

INGREDIENTS

2 pounds grass fed beef

1 cup converted long grain rice

1 onion, slivered

1 can garbanzo beans, drained

1 stick margarine

1 tsp each salt, cinnamon, all-spice and pepper

INSTRUCTIONS

Season meat and rice mixture with above seasonings in a bowl. Add slivered onions and garbanzo beans. Add one cup of water to one cup of rice. Melt butter and add to rice mixture.

Bake at 350 degrees in a deep metal pan. Cover with foil for one hour. Stir with fork. Lower heat to 250 degrees and bake for another 30 mins covered.

MIDDLE EASTERN GREEN BEANS

serves 6-8

INGREDIENTS

2 pounds of fresh green beans, rinsed and dried well

1 onion

2 cloves of garlic, crushed

1 tsp cinnamon

Salt and pepper to taste

1 tbsp cold-pressed olive oil

INSTRUCTIONS

Pinch ends off of green beans.

Saute onion in olive oil and garlic in saute pan. Add green beans.

Add some water so beans don't burn. Add seasonings.

Cover and let cook until beans are tender.

This side dish goes well with any meal!

BAKED ZUCCHINI FRIES

serves
4-6

INGREDIENTS

Cold pressed olive oil

4 medium sized zucchini

1 cup plain bread crumbs

1/4 cup freshly grated parmesan-
(omit for dairy-free)

1 teaspoon garlic powder

1/2 teaspoon ground paprika

1/8 tsp dried oregano

1/8 tsp crushed red pepper

1 tsp salt and pepper

2 large eggs

INSTRUCTIONS

Preheat oven to 425. Line 2 cookie sheets with parchment paper and brush paper with olive oil. Cut zucchini into fries. In a shallow dish, combine the breadcrumbs and dry ingredients. In a separate shallow dish, beat eggs.

Dip each piece into the egg mixture then into the bread crumb mixture and place on coikie sheet.

Once coated, spray the fries with olive oil. Bake for 20 minutess or until golden brown and crispy.

Serve with marinara sauce.

JEANNETTE'S COCONUT CAKE
A FAVORITE AT PARTIES!

serves
15-20

INGREDIENTS

1 package butter cake mix

ICING:

2 cups sugar

1 16-oz pkg low fat sour cream

1 12-oz frozen coconut

1 container whipped topping

INSTRUCTIONS

Bake cake as directed on box. Let cool.

Split into 2 layers using a string.

Mix sugar, sour cream and coconut together.

Reserve 1 cup of this mixture and spread the rest between layers of cake.

Combine the reserved 1 cup of mixture with 1 ½ cup of whipped topping and spread on top and sides of cake.

Refrigerate after icing cake.

serves
6–8

RUZ BI HALEEB (RICE MILK)
SO DELICIOUS!

INGREDIENTS

1 qt organic skim milk

2/3 cup white rice

1/2 stick butter

3 tbsp of Rose Water (available at international grocery store)

1/2 cup of sugar to taste

INSTRUCTIONS

Pour milk in pot. Bring to a boil.

Add rinsed and dried rice, butter and sugar.

Cook on low heat until rice is done.

Add the rose water, and stir well.

Pour into bowl and let cool.

SUMBOSI
LEBANESE COOKIES

makes 35-40

INGREDIENTS

1 cup cream wheat

2 cups flour

1/2 stick butter

2 cups of pecans

1 tsp sugar

FILLING

1/2 lb ground pecans

3/4 cup sugar

1 cup Rose Water (available in international groceries)

SIMPLE SYRUP

1 cup of sugar

1 cup of water

INSTRUCTIONS

COOKIES: Mix cream of wheat and flour well, add butter and 1 cup of hot water. Knead well until smooth. Cover with a dish cloth.

Roll into small balls. Poke a hole in each cookie, to hold filling. Add filling (below) into hole and pinch to close. Bake on cookie sheet lined with foil at 400 degrees until light brown.

FILLING: Combine ingredients at left in saucepan. Cook on low heat, do not stir often.

SIMPLE SYRUP: Combine sugar and water, boil. Cook until syrup is stringy. Add 1 tbsp of Rose Water. Dip each Sumbosi in the syrup and arrange -- not touching each other -- in a pan to cool.

SITIE QUINNIE'S FLAKY PIE CRUST

INGREDIENTS

2 cups flour
3/4 cup shortening
1/2 tsp salt
6 tbsp cold water

INSTRUCTIONS

Blend flour and shortening. Dissolve salt in cold water. Sprinkle over flour and shortening mixture. Mix well. Roll out on floured surface with rolling pin.

The secret of this tender crust is dissolving the salt in cold water. Bake single crust in 400 degree oven.

BERRY COBBLER

INGREDIENTS

2 pints strawberries, quartered
1 pint of blueberries
1 cup of sugar (divided)
1 tbsp cornstarch
3/4 cup flour
1 tsp baking powder
1/2 tsp salt
1 egg
1/4 cup organic skim milk
1/2 tsp vanilla extract
6 tbsp butter, melted

INSTRUCTIONS

Preheat oven to 375 degrees.

Combine berries, 1/3 cup plus of 2 tsp sweetener and cornstarch. Let stand for 10 minutes.

In another bowl, mix flour, ½ the sweetener, baking powder and salt.

In a third bowl, stir egg, milk, vanilla and butter. Add dry ingredients. Stir well. Place six 6 oz. ramekins on a baking sheet. Divide fruit evenly and top each with a few spoonfuls of batter. Bake 25-30 minutes until golden brown. Cool and serve.

CRAWFISH CHOWDER

serves
8-10

INGREDIENTS

1 lb frozen, peeled Louisiana crawfish

1 stick butter

2 tsp flour

1/2 cup onion, chopped

1 can cream-style corn

1/2 tsp Worcestershire sauce

2 cups low fat milk

INSTRUCTIONS

In a deep pot, melt butter and add flour. Stir to blend, then saute onions in the butter and flour mixture until transluscent.

Add 2 cups of milk, Worcestershire, cream-style corn and crawfish.

Let simmer for one hour or until chowder thickens.

CRABMEAT DIP

INGREDIENTS

1 green bell pepper, finely chopped

2 pimentos, finely chopped

1 tbsp English mustard

1 tsp salt

1/2 tsp white pepper

2 eggs, beaten

1 cup light mayo

3 lb lump crabmeat

INSTRUCTIONS

Mix pepper and pimentos, add mustard, salt, eggs and mayo. Mix well. Add crab-meat and mix with fingers all lumps are broken up.

Divide mixture into 8 crab shells or rame-kins. Top with light mayo and sprinkle with paprika.

Bake at 350 degrees for 15 minutes.

Serve hot or cold with melba rounds. This also makes a great filling for mini-quiche or puff pastry shells.

COCKTAIL SAUCE FOR SHRIMP AND CRAB

serves 6-8

INGREDIENTS

2 cup ketchup

1/4 cup cider vinegar

1/4 cup minced onion

1/2 cup prepared horseradish

1 tsp hot mustard

2 cup chili sauce

6 drops of hot sauce

2 tbsp Worcestershire sauce

INSTRUCTIONS

Put all ingredients in blender, process until well blended.

Refrigerate until serving.

Serve with chilled shrimp and crab.

AUNT LAURENCE'S CRAWFISH ÉTOUFFÉE

serves 8–10

INGREDIENTS

2 pounds Louisiana Crawfish

1 stick butter

1 cup celery, chopped

1 large onion, chopped

1 large green bell pepper, chopped

2 cans of Cream of Mushroom soup (can substitute with low fat version)

4-5 green onion tops, chopped

1-2 cans of water

1 tbsp Worcestershire Sauce

salt and red pepper to taste

INSTRUCTIONS

Thaw packages of frozen crawfish in cold water. Melt butter in medium size pot, add onion, celery and bell pepper. Saute until tender. Add crawfish, cans of soup and water. Consistency should be like a thick sauce - not a soup. Add flour to thicken if needed. Add seasonings and Worcestershire sauce.

Cover and let cook on low fire for about one hour.

Serve over rice with French bread and garnish with green onion tops.

ITALIAN SAUSAGE ON A BROWN GRAVY

serves
8

INGREDIENTS

3 pounds Italian chicken sausage

2 packets Brown Gravy Mix (follow instructions on packet)

1 large onion, chopped

1 green bell pepper, chopped

1½ tsp canola oil

INSTRUCTIONS

Heat oil in large skillet then brown sausage for about 5 minutes on each side.

Add onion, celery and bell pepper and gravy.

If needed, add ½ cup of flour to thicken. Stir well until flour is transparent.

Simmer and cover for 1 ½ hours. Serve over brown or white rice, with a green salad.

LOUISIANA SOUTHERN-STYLE RIBS

serves
6-8

INGREDIENTS

Ribs - pork or beef

Dry rub (brown sugar, paprika, Cajun seasoning, garlic powder and onion powder)

1 cup of BBQ sauce

1/2 cup Worcestershire sauce

INSTRUCTIONS

Preheat oven to 300. Cover meaty side of ribs with Worcestershire and dry rub. Sear on grill for about 5 minutes on each side. Remove and baste with bbq sauce. Wrap tightly in foil and place on cookie sheet. Place in oven for one hour then baste again. Bake for another 1 ½ hour until meat falls off the bone. Serve with Toni's Rice Dressing (recipe pg 36) and corn on the cob.

CAJUN CHICKEN AND SAUSAGE JAMBALAYA

serves
8-10

INGREDIENTS

1¼ cup rice

2½ cups low sodium chicken broth

1 large onion, chopped

1 large green bell pepper, chopped

2 celery stalks, chopped

3 cloves garlic, minced

1 pound of boneless, skinless chicken breasts

1 can crushed tomatoes

2 tbsp canola oil

salt and pepper

2 tsp Worcestershire sauce

1/2 tsp hot sauce, optional

INSTRUCTIONS

Heat 2 tsp oil in large Dutch oven over medium heat. Season sausage and chicken with salt and pepper. Saute' sausage until brown. Remove from heat.

Add one tsp of oil and saute chicken pieces until brown on both sides. Remove and set aside.

In the same pot, saute onion, bell pepper, celery and garlic until tender. Stir in crushed tomatoes and season with red and black pepper, Worcestershire and Tabasco. Stir in chicken and sausage.

Cook for 10 minutes.

Stir in rice and chicken broth and bring to a boil.

Reduce heat and simmer for 20-25 minutes, or until liquid is absorbed.

SHRIMP FETUCCINE

INGREDIENTS

2 pounds shrimp
2 onions, chopped
2 bell peppers, chopped
2 celery stalks, chopped
2 garlic cloves, minced
2 sticks butter
1/4 cup flour
1 pt half-and-half (reg or fat-free)
1 package of fettucine (cooked)
1 lb pepper cheese
1 cup cheddar cheese

INSTRUCTIONS

Saute onions, pepper, celery and garlic in butter.

Add flour, the half-and-half and cheese.

Add shrimp and cooked pasta.

Mix all ingredients well in a large pot.

Pour into a greased 9x12" baking dish and sprinkle with cheddar cheese.

Bake at 350 until bubbly and golden brown, about 30 minutes.

CHICKEN FRICASSEE

serves
6-8

INGREDIENTS

1 large chicken, cut up

2 large onions, chopped

1 cup canola oil

1 cup flour

salt and pepper to taste

parsley and shallot tops

INSTRUCTIONS

Clean chicken well. Dredge each piece in flour and brown in oil in a large, deep pot.

Remove chicken and brown onions in the oil.

Add chicken back into the pot and add about 1 ½ qts of water. Let cook until chicken is tender, stirring to be sure it does not stick. Gravy should be thick.

Ten minutes before serving, add chopped parsley and onion tops.

Serve over white or brown rice. Serve with cucumber, tomato, avocado salad (toss with vinegar, olive oil and a dash of sugar).

SEAFOOD GUMBO

serves 10-15

INGREDIENTS

3 tbsp canola oil

3 tbsp flour

1 large onion, chopped

1 green bell pepper, chopped

2-3 cloves garlic, minced

3 qt water

salt, red and black pepper (to taste)

1 can crabmeat and several whole crabs

1 lb shrimp, peeled

1 small container oysters with liquid

1/2 cup fresh parsley, chopped without stems

3 ribs celery, chopped

INSTRUCTIONS

In a large stock pot, make a roux with the oil and flour. Cook slowly, stirring often until brown.

Add onion, celery and bell pepper to the roux. Slowly add 3 qts of water, stirring while you pour. Add salt and pepper to taste.

Add fresh crabmeat and several whole crabs. Cook for about one hour. Add shrimp and liquid from oysters and cook until shrimp are done.

Add chopped parsley and green onions about 30 minutes before serving. About 15 mins before serving, add the oysters.

Serve over rice, with sliced French bread.

Note: To save time, use packaged Dry Roux mix (available online). See Chicken and Sausage Gumbo recipe (page 56) for instructions, or see back of jar.

CHICKEN AND SAUSAGE GUMBO

serves
10-15

INGREDIENTS

2 large onions, chopped

2 green bell peppers, chopped

4 stalks celery, chopped

4 heaping tbsp Dry Roux mix (available online)

4 cups boiling water

2 packages turkey, andouille or smoked sausage, sliced

1/2 cup flour

2 tbsp canola oil

1 pkg chicken thighs with bone, remove skin

Salt and red pepper to taste

INSTRUCTIONS

Add oil to large, deep pot on medium heat.

Add chopped vegetables and saute until tender. Add the roux mix to boiling water and whisk until well blended. Add to pot with vegetables.

Add the flour and whisk in pot until flour is well blended with roux.

Rinse and season chicken with salt and pepper and add into pot. Add sausage.

Season entire pot with salt and pepper. Cover and cook on low-medium heat. Let cook for 2-3 hours until chicken is done and falls off the bone. Remove bones from the gumbo.

Serve over rice with French Bread.

Optional: add Gumbo File (available at most grocery stores) and hot sauce to add a kick to the finished product! Note: This can be made in a slow cooker as well.

SHRIMP AND CRAB AU GRATIN

serves 8-10

INGREDIENTS

2 large onions, chopped

3 ribs of celery, chopped

1/2 stick of butter

4 tbsp flour

1 large and 1 small can of evaporated milk

2 egg yolks

1 lb of fresh crabmeat

1 lb of peeled, chopped shrimp

1 cup of grated parmesan cheese

INSTRUCTIONS

Saute onions and celery in butter until soft.

Add flour and blend with milk.

Remove from heat, add egg yolks, crabmeat and shrimp, salt and pepper.

Add grated cheese to top of casserole.

Place in a greased casserole dish and bake at 350 for 15-20 minutes.

RED BEANS AND TURKEY SAUSAGE

serves
8-10

INGREDIENTS

1 package navy beans or beans of your choice

1 onion, chopped

1 green bell pepper, chopped

2 cloves of garlic, chopped

1 package Onion Soup Mix

2 packs turkey sausage, sliced (skinless turkey sausage is best) or sausage of your choice

INSTRUCTIONS

Rinse beans well. Pour them into slow cooker. Add 2 ½ cups of water. (I usually just measure to halfway - you can always add more. You don't want them too soupy).

Add the chopped onion, garlic and bell pepper and soup mix. Stir well then add sausage.

Cover and cook on high for at least 3 hours. Then turn to low. Once beans become soft, mash up against the sides with spoon to make them creamy. Continue this for duration of cooking. Let cook for about 6 hours. Serve with rice.

JEANNETTE'S COUNTRY OVEN RIBS

serves 6-8

INGREDIENTS

2 lb country ribs
1/2 each tsp salt and pepper
1 tsp mustard
1/2 tsp garlic powder
1 tsp sugar
1 cup ketchup
1/2 cup Worcestershire
1 large onion, sliced

INSTRUCTIONS

Preheat oven to 350.

Season each rib with dry ingredients.

Slice onion in rounds and place on each rib.

Bake in oven, uncovered, for 45 minutes or until tender.

When ribs are done, baste BBQ sauce all over and bake another 20-30 minutes longer.

BAKED OYSTERS

serves
4-6

INGREDIENTS

1/4 cup butter
1/4 cup olive oil
2/3 cup Italian bread crumbs
1/2 tsp salt
1/2 tsp ground black pepper
2 tbsp chopped green onion tops
1/8 tsp cayenne pepper
1/2 cup dried tarragon
1/2 tsp oregano
2 tbsp parsley, minced
1½ pints oysters
Melba rounds

INSTRUCTIONS

Preheat oven to 450 degrees.

In a saucepan, melt butter over low heat.

Mix in olive oil and butter.

Add remaining ingredients, except oysters and melba rounds. Mix well. Remove pan from heat.

Place well drained oysters in an ovenproof serving dish. Cover with sauce.

Bake for 20 minutes or until top is lightly browned. Serve with melba rounds.

SEAFOOD AND EGGPLANT CASSEROLE

serves
8 - 10

INGREDIENTS

2 large eggplants, peeled and finely chopped

1/3 cup onions, chopped

1/2 cup celery, chopped

1/2 cup bell pepper, chopped

1lb peeled medium sized shrimp

1/2 lb fresh crabmeat

1/2 lb butter

1/2 cup bread crumbs

salt and pepper to taste

INSTRUCTIONS

Cook eggplant, onion, celery and bell pepper in butter on low heat for about 1 ½ hours in a medium saucepan on stove top. DO NOT BROWN.

Add shrimp and crabmeat, and continue to cook until shrimp is cooked (about 10 minutes).

Remove from heat. Add salt and pepper and bread crumbs. Pour into a 9x12" glass casserole dish.

Bake for 25 minutes at 350 degrees, until bread crumbs are brown.

Freezes well for later use, if needed.

Serve with a salad.

TROUT ALMANDINE

serves
4

INGREDIENTS

4 trout fillets

1/2 - 3/4 cup butter

3/4 cup flour

juice of one lemon

salt and pepper to taste

1 cup slivered almonds

INSTRUCTIONS

Rinse fish and pat dry with paper towels.

In a large skillet over medium heat, melt butter.

Dredge trout in flour. Sprinkle with lemon juice, salt and pepper. Pan fry for 5 minutes per side until crispy.

Remove from pan and keep warm.

Add almonds to butter and saute 1-2 minutes. Pour over trout before serving.

SAUTEED CAJUN REDFISH

serves
4

INGREDIENTS

4 redfish fillets
2 tbsp fish rub (below)
1/2 cup flour
1 egg, beaten
1/4 cup water
1/3 cup canola oil

FISH RUB:

5 tbsp black pepper
6 tbsp garlic powder
3 tbsp onion powder
6 tbsp salt
2½ tbsp dried oregano
1-2 tbsp red pepper

INSTRUCTIONS

Combine ingredients for Fish Rub. Store in a airtight container for no longer than 3 months.

Season fillets with 1 tbsp rub.

In a shallow bowl, combine flour with 2 tsp of rub mixture.

In another bowl, mix egg, water and remaining rub mixture.

Dredge fillets in seasoned flour then egg mixture, then again in flour, shaking off any excess.

In a large nonstick skillet, over medium heat, heat oil. Pan fry fillets for 4-5 minutes on each side till crispy. Drain well on paper towels. Serve hot.

Note: You can substitute with red snapper, rainbow trout or grouper.

MACQUE CHOUX

serves 6-8

INGREDIENTS

6 cups fresh or frozen corn

1 onion, chopped

1 green bell pepper, chopped

3 large tomatoes, peeled and chopped

2 tbsp extra virgin olive oil

1 tsp each: salt and sugar

1/2 tsp black pepper

INSTRUCTIONS

Cut corn off the cob, making sure to cut the kernel in half and scrape off the cob.

Heat oil in saucepan, add onion. Once onion is transparent, add green peppers, tomatoes, corn and seasoning.

Cook over medium heat, stirring frequently. Let simmer for about one hour.

SITIE QUINNIE'S CORNBREAD DRESSING

 serves 8

INGREDIENTS

2 boxes of cornbread (Bake according to box and in 9x12 baking dish)

2 onions, chopped

2 green bell peppers, chopped

1 cup of celery, chopped

2 cups of chicken broth

¼ cup margarine

INSTRUCTIONS

Note: Prepare cornbread day before making dressing. Preheat oven to 350 degrees. Crumble cornbread. Saute onion, bell pepper and celery in margarine. Once tender, add to cornbread mixture. Add chicken broth and spices. Add more chicken broth as needed if too thick. Bake for 45 minutes or until golden brown. Stir. You want cornbread to be moist, not runny or dry.

HASH BROWN CASSEROLE

serves
6-8

INGREDIENTS

1 package frozen hash browns

3/4 cup butter, melted

1/2 cup chopped onioin

1 can low fat Cream of Mushroom soup

1 8 oz container low fat sour cream

1 cup shredded cheese

2 cup corn flakes

INSTRUCTIONS

Combine potatoes, ½ cup of the butter, onions, soup, sour cream and cheese. Stir well.

Spoon into a greased 2 ½ qt. casserole dish.

Crush corn flakes and stir in remaining butter. Sprinkle over potato mixture.

Bake at 350 for 50 minutes.

serves
6

SWEET POTATO CASSEROLE

INGREDIENTS

5-6 sweet potatoes

1 small can condensed milk

1/2 tsp each: cinnamon, nutmeg and allspice

1 cup pecans, chopped

1 pkg mini marshmallows

1 egg, beaten

INSTRUCTIONS

Boil potatoes until soft. When cool, peel and mash.

Using a hand mixer, add egg, milk and spices. Fold in chopped pecans.

Bake at 350 degrees for 25 minutes. Top with marshmallows and brown lightly.

GARLIC CHEESE GRITS

serves 8-10

INGREDIENTS

1 cup grits, uncooked

4 cup water

1 tbsp salt

2 tbsp Worcestershire

1 stick butter

1 small package pepper cheese

1/2 lb sharp cheddar cheese

INSTRUCTIONS

Cook grits in salted water.

When cooked, add butter, Velveeta, cheddar cheese and Worcestershire.

Stir until butter and cheese have melted.

Put in a greased casserole dish and sprinkle with paprika. Bake in preheated oven at 350 degrees for 15-20 minutes.

BROWNIE SHEET CAKE

serves
1-20

INGREDIENTS, CAKE

2 cups of sugar
2 cups of flour
1/2 cup margarine
1/2 cup canola oil
4 tbsp cocoa
1 cup water
1/2 cup buttermilk
2 eggs
1 tsp vanilla
1 tsp baking soda

INGREDIENTS, FROSTING

1/2 cup margarine
4 tbsp cocoa
1/2 cup nonfat milk
1 box powdered sugar
1/4 tsp vanilla
1/2 cup pecans, chopped

INSTRUCTIONS

CAKE: Preheat oven to 400 degrees.

Sift 2 cups of sugar and flour, set aside.

In a saucepan, combine ½ c margarine, oil, 4 tbsp cocoa and water. Bring to a boil and pour over flour mixture and stir.

Add buttermilk, eggs, 1 tsp of vanilla and baking soda. Mix well.

Pour batter into a greased pan and bake for 20 minutes.

FROSTING: combine margarine, cocoa and milk in a saucepan. Bring to a boil. Remove from heat.

Add powdered sugar and vanilla. Beat until smooth.

Stir in pecans and spread over hot cake.

NEW ORLEANS PRALINES

makes
24

INGREDIENTS

2 cups sugar

1 cup brown sugar

1 cup evaporated milk

4 cup pecans

1 tsp vanilla

3/4 stick butter

INSTRUCTIONS

Combine sugars, cream and butter, slowly bring to a boil.

Cook until soft ball stage (234 to 241° F).

Remove from heat and beat -- by hand with a fork -- rapidly for about 1 minute until sugars are well blended. Add vanilla and pecans. Drop by spoon onto aluminum foil and let cool.

APPLE DUMPLINGS
MY MOTHER'S FAVORITE!

makes 16

INGREDIENTS

2 Granny Smith apples

2 cans Pillsbury (R) Crescent Rolls

1 litre bottle 7-Up (R)

2 cups sugar

2 sticks butter

Dash vanilla

Pinch salt

1/2 tsp cinnamon

INSTRUCTIONS

Peel and slice apples into 8 pieces. Prep a 9x13" baking dish with cooking spray. Place one apple slice on each crescent, roll up and place on cookie sheet. Sprinkle cinnamon over dumplings.

Melt butter in saucepan. Add sugar and vanilla. Stir well. Spoon butter / sugar mixture over rolls and add a capful of 7-Up to each dumpling. Bake at 350 for 35-40 minutes. Let stand in pan before serving. Great with ice cream!

AUNT JUANITA'S ALMOND BARK

serves **14-16**

INGREDIENTS

10 cups Rice Chex (R) cereal

15 oz pecans and peanuts

2 pkg almond bark

INSTRUCTIONS

Mix dry ingredients on cookie sheet covered with foil, melt bark and pour over mixture. Mix well.

After it cools and hardens, break into chunks. Great during the holidays!

CHOCOLATE SOUFFLÉ

serves
6

INGREDIENTS

4 tbsp butter

4 tbsp flour

1½ cup milk

3 squares unsweetened baking chocolate

2/3 cup sugar

4 tbsp hot water

6 eggs, separated

1 tsp vanilla

INSTRUCTIONS

In a saucepan, melt butter and add flour.

Slowly add milk while stirring constantly. Cook to boiling point.

Melt chocolate over hot water, add sugar and 4 tbsp hot water. Stir until smooth.

Combine mixtures, add well-beaten egg yolks. Let cool. Whip egg whites and fold into chocolate mixture. Add vanilla.

Bake at 325 for 45 minutes. Serve with whipped cream if desired.

LEMON ICE BOX PIE

makes
1 9"
pie

INGREDIENTS, PIE

3 egg yolks

1 small can sweetened condensed milk

1/2 cup fresh lemon juice

1 Graham cracker crust

Perfect Meringue (recipe at right)

INGREDIENTS, MERINGUE

3 egg whites

1/2 tsp vanilla

1/4 tsp cream of tartar

6 tbsp sugar

INSTRUCTIONS

Preheat oven to 350.

Lightly beat egg yolks.

Add milk and lemon juice. Mix thoroughly.

Pour into pie crust. Top with Perfect Meringue. Bake 12-15 minutes or until lightly browned. Refrigerate.

Meringue: In a deep bowl, beat egg whites with vanilla and cream of tartar. Add sugar gradually, beating until stiff glossy peaks form and sugar is dissolved.

MISSISSIPPI MUDCAKE

serves
12-20

INGREDIENTS, CAKE

1 cup margarine

1/2 cup cocoa

2 cups of sugar

1½ cup flour

1 cup pecans, chopped

1 cup coconut

4 eggs

7 oz pkg miniature marshmallows

INGREDIENTS, ICING

1/2 cup margarine

1/2 cup cocoa

1 box powdered sugar

1/2 cup evaporated milk

INSTRUCTIONS

Preheat oven to 350.

Melt margarine and place in a large bowl. Separately add cocoa, sugar, flour, pecans, coconut and eggs, beating well after each addition.

Pour mixture into a greased 13x9" baking pan.

Bake for 35-45 minutes.

In a saucepan, mix icing ingredients. Heat to a boil. Simmer until ready to use.

Remove cake from oven. Immediately top with marshmallows. Pour hot icing over cake.

Enjoy!